FIRST AMERICANS

The Navajo

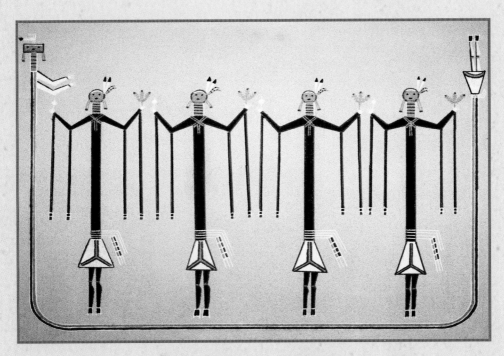

DAVID C. KING

Marshall Cavendish
Benchmark
New York

ACKNOWLEDGMENTS

Series consultant: Raymond Bial

Benchmark Books
Marshall Cavendish
99 White Plains Road
Tarrytown, New York 10591
www.marshallcavendish.us

Text copyright © 2006 by Marshall Cavendish Corporation
Map and illustrations copyright © 2006 by Marshall Cavendish Corporation

All Internet sites were available and accurate when sent to press.

Library of Congress Cataloging-in-Publication Data
King, David C.
The Navajo / by David C. King.
p. cm. — (First Americans)
Summary: "General overview for young readers of the Navajo people. Covers history, daily life, and beliefs.
Includes bibliographical references and index.
ISBN 0-7614-1897-0
1. Navajo Indians—History—Juvenile literature. 2. Navajo Indians—Social life and customs—Juvenile literature. I. Title. II. Series:
First Americans (Benchmark Books) (Firm)
E99.N3K44 2005
979.1004'9726—dc22
2004027572

On the cover: A Navajo girl in traditional dress.

Title page: Navajo sand painting with theme of abundance.

Photo Research by Joan Meisel

The photographs in this book are used by permission and through the courtesy of: Cover photo: Art Stein/Photo Researchers, Inc.
Bruce Coleman, Inc.: Wolfgang Bayer, 4; *Corbis*: Geoffrey Clements, 1, 28; George H. H. Huey, 6, 16, 30; David Muench, 7; Bettmann, 12;
Pete Saloutos, 14; Kevin Fleming, 20, 36, 39; Ric Ergenbright, 24; Ted Spiegel, 26; Neil Rabinowitz, 34. *Getty Images*: David McNew, 40;
North Wind Picture Archives: 11, 21. *Photo Researchers, Inc.*:Don Getsug, 18; Paolo Koch, 22. *Peter Arnold*:Weatherstock, 32.

Map and illustrations by Christopher Santoro
Series design by Symon Chow

Printed in China
1 3 5 6 4 2

CONTENTS

1 · THE LAND AND THE PEOPLE

The Navajo people believe that everything is alive and has a spirit, or soul—even rocks and clouds, snowstorms and caterpillars. The Navajo homeland, now the Navajo **Reservation**, in the American Southwest in many ways looks like an enchanted land. A land where rock has been carved by years of wind and rain. It is a place where towering mountains rise from the desert floor, their peaks capped with snow above mountainsides thick with pine trees. Cinnamon-red canyons and springtime wildflowers gleam under deep blue skies and puffy white clouds.

The Navajo Reservation is a harsh land. It is so dry that most streams, called **washes**, have no water most of the year. When the spring rains come, the washes turn into swift rivers. Many kinds of animals are able to live here, including rattlesnakes,

Two Navajo children near their home in Monument Valley, Arizona.

jackrabbits, horned toads, and, in the mountains, bears and mountain lions.

The Navajo call their homeland **Dinetah.** This means home of **Diné**, which is the Navajo word meaning "the people." It is the largest Indian reservation in the nation, covering about 16 million acres. It covers more land than Massachusetts, Connecticut, and Vermont combined. This

The Navajo have lived in Canyon de Chelly since the 1700s. The canyon is now a national park in the state of Arizona.

huge reservation covers a large area of Arizona, and corners of New Mexico, and Utah. Two hundred thousand Navajo live on the reservation.

Navajo history goes back thousands of years. Their ancestors came from Asia. Over many centuries, these Asian people moved south and spread out over North and South America.

Navajo drawings at Canyon de Chelly show the arrival of Spaniards on horseback.

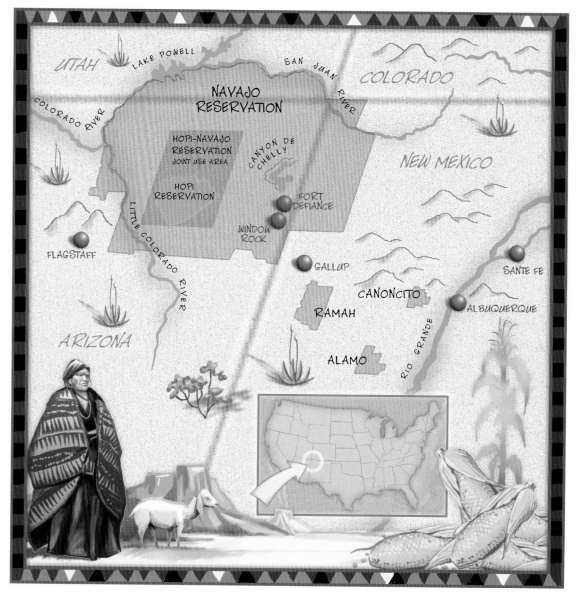

This map shows Navajo Reservations. The largest reservation covers lands in Utah, Arizona, and New Mexico. The Hopi Reservation lies within this area. Other Navajo lands are in the towns of Ramah, Alamo, and Canoncito, New Mexico.

About seven hundred years ago, the ancestors of today's Navajo moved to the land they call Dinetah. They lived by hunting and by gathering wild foods. But they saw that people living near them had a more comfortable life by farming. These neighbors, called the Pueblo, grew corn, squash, beans, and sunflowers. The Navajo quickly learned to be skilled farmers.

About 350 years ago the Spanish moved into what is now the American Southwest. The Spanish brought horses into the region, and also other animals—sheep, goats, and cattle. The Navajo quickly became skilled riders and trainers of horses. They also became herders of sheep and learned to weave the wool into beautiful blankets and clothing.

The Spanish wanted to take over Navajo lands. At times, Navajo warriors joined with the Pueblos and drove the Spanish out. But the Spanish kept coming back. In 1821 Mexico won its independence from Spain and took over Spain's empire in North America. But Mexican control did not last long. The United States defeated Mexico in a war and gained all of the Southwest and California in 1848.

The Navajo soon found themselves fighting the American government and settlers who wanted to take over their lands. Open warfare broke out in 1863. To win what were called the Navajo Wars, the U.S. government placed a tough frontiersman named Colonel Christopher "Kit" Carson in charge of a group of volunteer soldiers.

Kit Carson defeated one warrior band after another, and forced the rest of the people to surrender. The soldiers then made the Navajo march more than 300 miles (480 km) to a barren stretch of land called the **Bosque Redondo**. Carson's men destroyed the Navajo's homes, most of their sheep and cattle, and their peach orchards. Several hundred Navajo people died on the trail they still call the **Long Walk**.

The Navajo suffered for four years at the Bosque Redondo. The land was poor and the crops failed. The people suffered from cold and hunger. About two thousand Navajo people died during this time. Several hundred escaped back to their canyons. Shortly before he died, Carson realized that Bosque Redondo was a mistake. He helped to convince the U.S. government to end the Navajo's time there. In 1868 a treaty was signed that allowed them to return to their homeland, which now became the Navajo Reservation.

Starting over after 1868 was not easy. The Navajo had few sheep or other animals. Their trees and their homes

Christopher "Kit" Carson led U.S. volunteer soldiers in the Navajo Wars.

One of the Navajo warriors who fought the American troops in the Navajo Wars was Barboncito. Even after surrendering, he never stopped working for the freedom of his people. In 1868 the government tried to move the Navajo to Oklahoma Territory, where land was set aside for them. In a powerful speech, Barboncito said, "We do not want to go to the right or to the left, but straight back to our own country." In return, Barboncito and other tribal leaders promised never to fight the United States again. The government released the Navajo, and the Navajo kept their promise not to fight.

were destroyed. Slowly, the Navajo worked to make their home what it once was. Oil was discovered on the reservation in 1921, and a **Tribal Council** was formed to protect the rights of the many families and clans. But money made from oil and minerals on the reservation was not enough to bring the Navajo out of poverty.

2 · THE NAVAJO WAY OF LIFE

A Navajo woman named Bit-so, which means "soft feather," told of growing up in a traditional Navajo family. "The family is everything to the Navajo, and the mother is the most important person. Years later, when I married, we stayed with my mother's clan, or group of families. My father belonged to a different clan." Today there are more than sixty clans making up the Navajo Nation.

Bit-so continued: "Our family taught us all the Navajo stories and they taught us the things we needed to know to be a help." By the time she was twelve years old, Bit-so could tend the corn and other crops, make use of wild plants and herbs, prepare meals, make baskets, spin wool into yarn, and weave

A Navajo shepherdess gathers her sheep.

This rug depicts daily life on the Navajo Reservation.

a small rug. "My brothers also learned from my father and uncles, but they never seemed to work as hard as the girls. They tended the flocks of sheep and goats, took care of the horses, and went along on hunting trips. The two hard things they did were to draw water from the river and gather firewood. Both those tasks took strength and a lot of walking."

A traditional Navajo house is called a **hogan**. It is built a certain way because the Navajo believe that the design was created long ago by **First Man** and **First Woman**. The hogan is a place of worship as well as a home.

While there are some differences in size and shape, most hogans today are built of logs. The dome-shaped roof is covered with red claylike mud. There is only one door to a hogan, and it always faces east toward the morning sun. Sometimes the doorway is covered with a mat rather than a wooden door. There are no windows, and only a few sheepskins and blankets, clothing, and cooking materials inside.

When a new hogan is built, a Navajo singer leads a special ceremony called the **Blessingway**. This is to bring happiness to all who live there. Today, many Navajo live in typical American houses or mobile homes, but some families still live in traditional hogans. Because the space is small, family members are careful to respect each other's place.

A Navajo woman and child near their hogan.

Some Navajo Words and Phrases

What would it be like to speak in the Navajo language? Here's your chance to try. The words and phrases below have been spelled the way they sound. Try saying some phrases with a friend.

Navajo	English
Yin-ish-ye _____.	My name is _____.
Ooshdla.	I believe it.
Hashni-nit.	Let me tell you something.
Ooj-onli.	I hope it is delightful.
Ch-eeh deya.	I am tired. Or, I am exhausted.
T-oo afini.	You are joking.
Hoz-hoo-niish hani baa?	Is it good news?
Yish-diah.	I am laughing.

Women always sit against the north wall, while men sit against the south. Children are always near their mother, and elders have a seat of honor on the west wall, facing the doorway.

During the hot summer months, the Navajo build a shelter of upright poles covered with branches called a **ramada**, which means shade.

A farm field on the Navajo Reservation. The Navajo learned farming from their neighbors the Pueblo Indians.

Hunting is still an important part of the Navajo way of life. Boys learn to hunt deer and small animals. They also learn to take only as much as they need for their family.

Corn has always been important to the Navajo. It is dried and then ground into cornmeal. The cornmeal is used to make tortillas, tamales, corn cakes, soup, and mush. Corn dishes are often spiced with hot Mexican chili peppers.

Women often cook over an open fire in the yard. In

A Navajo family with their blanket loom.

cold weather, Navajo who live in hogans cook inside. Smoke escapes through a hole in the roof. Beans, squash, and different kinds of breads are all favorite foods.

Women not only prepared all the meals, but made the family's clothing as well. The Navajo once made their clothing from deerskin and the hides of other animals. When they learned about sheep and wool from the Spanish, they

A Navajo woman spins wool to be used on her loom.

began weaving woolen garments. They also learned about cotton clothing from the Pueblo.

During the 1800s, the wives of U.S. Army officers gave the Navajo dresses and fabrics. Over their dresses, Navajo women often wear woven shawls, called **mantas**. They borrowed this idea from the Mexican people.

Men and boys also borrowed clothing styles from the Pueblos, Mexicans, Spanish, and Americans. A style that is still common is a loose shirt and white, calf-length pants, along with headbands of twisted cloth. They also copied a Mexican style of draping a Navajo blanket over one shoulder. Today, men, women, and children are likely to wear T-shirts and jeans, but the traditional styles are still popular.

Navajo Crafts

The Navajo people are famous throughout the world for their outstanding skill in two crafts: wool weaving and jewelry making. Navajo women have always been the great weavers, while jewelry has usually been made by men.

Navajo women learned to weave from the Pueblo Indians who had been taught by the Spanish. The Navajo were soon known as the most skilled weavers in North America.

After the sheep were sheared, women washed the wool in suds made from crushed yucca roots. They next combed, or carded, the wool with two spiked boards, then twisted, or spun, it on a round spindle to make one long thread. Next came the long, slow work of weaving.

After several weeks of weaving, and about two hundred hours at the loom, a weaver would have a small rug or blanket, about 5 feet by 3 feet (1.5 by .90 m). The weav-

A woman wearing turquoise and silver jewelry clasps her hands over a traditional Navajo blanket.

ings are called blankets or rugs, but they can be used as shawls or wall hangings.

The Navajo developed their own designs in the late 1800s. Some designs have special meanings, like a zigzag pattern for lightning or layers of thick lines for clouds. The patterns, and the colors used, are sometimes named after the weaver's area of the reservation, such as Wide Ruins, Window Rock, or Two Gray Hills.

In the mid-1800s, the Navajo learned the art of making silver jewelry. Captain Henry L. Dodge, the U.S. government's Indian agent at Fort Defiance, brought a silversmith from Mexico to teach the skills to the Navajo. More and more men, and a few women, picked up the skills, and some added their knowledge of working with turquoise and other stones. Like the Navajo weavers, the jewelry makers were soon famous throughout the world for their large necklaces, buckles, bracelets, and other items.

3 · BELIEFS AND CEREMONIES

The Navajo believe that everything on earth has a spirit—plants and animals, rocks and soil, wind and rain. They want their lives to be in balance, or harmony, with the universe. People stay in harmony by living in a "good way." This means respecting others, respecting nature, and not doing things that might anger one of the **Holy People**. These bad things are called **taboos**. Killing a snake, eating raw meat, and stepping over a sleeping person are all taboos. Throughout their growing years, children learn the right ways of living from the Navajo stories told by family members.

The Navajo have many different rituals. A Blessingway ceremony is meant to bring good luck, good health, and blessings. Blessingways are held for mothers shortly before

A Navajo medicine man creates a sandpainting.

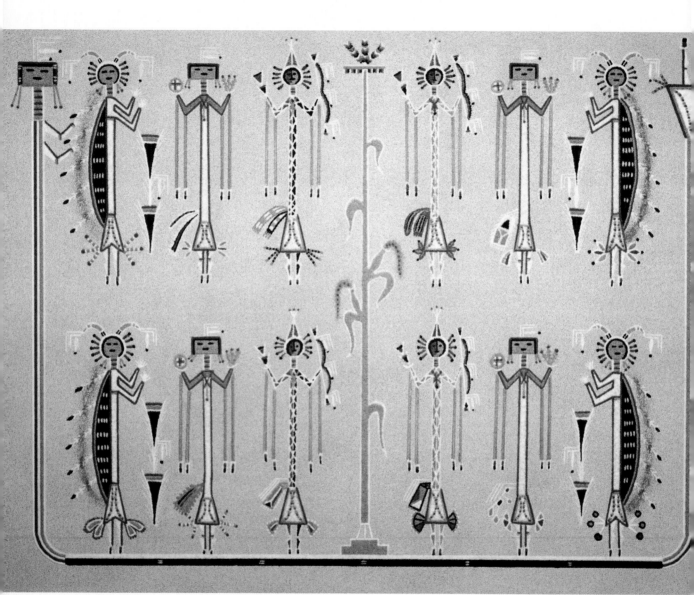

Some Navajo sandpaintings are made as part of healing ceremonies. Others are created as works of art using Navajo symbols.

giving birth, for young men leaving to join the armed forces, for a couple when they marry, and whenever someone needs good luck.

Another type of ceremony is the **chantway**. This is a healing ceremony led by a singer or medicine man. The purpose of the ceremony is to ask the Holy People to help drive out the evil spirit that has invaded the person's body. The ritual begins with a **sandpainting**, which is also known as a dry painting.

These are not really paintings, since powders are used instead of paint. The healer works on a large piece of deerskin, or on the level sand floor of a hogan. Although sandpaintings are beautiful, they are not made to last. They must be wiped away before dark, or at dawn if the sandpainting is made at night.

The healing ceremony can last from one to nine days, with a new drawing every day. The patient sits in the center of the sandpainting while family members and friends chant and dance outside the hogan. The healer also gives healing herbs to the sick person. If the person gets well, the Navajo say that harmony has been restored by the Holy People who drove out the evil spirit. If not, the

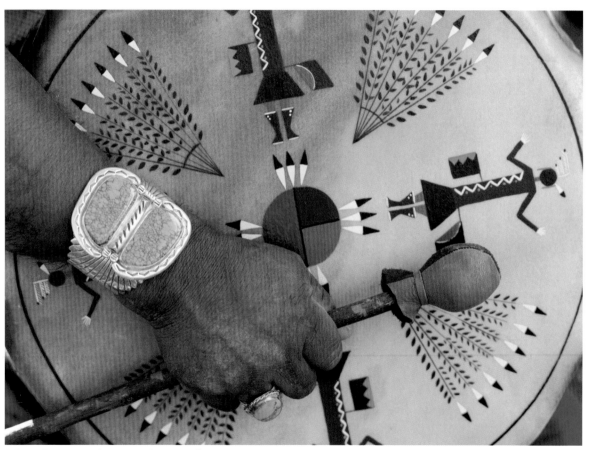

This drum is decorated with figures that represent traditional Navajo Holy People.

Navajo believe that it was the will of the Holy People.

Every phase of a Navajo's life is marked by special rituals. When a baby is born, it is placed on the mother's left side, with its head toward the north. A medicine man sprinkles the infant with corn pollen, the symbol of life.

When children are twelve or thirteen years old, they are welcomed into the tribe in a ceremony called *Yeibichai* (YAY-beh-cha-yee). Toward the end of the ceremony, two men in scary masks jump out at the children. The men then complete their dance and remove the masks so that the children can see that the men are family members. The children then put on the masks to show that they are no longer afraid of scary things.

In traditional Navajo families, when a young couple wants to marry, there is great joy and excitement because it creates the promise of more children. The future groom brings an expensive gift to his bride's family. In the past, the gift would be a deer; in modern times, a horse.

The Story of Creation

There are more than fifty versions of the Navajo creation story. Here is the basic story:

In the beginning, the earth's creatures lived in darkness, some say deep inside the earth. These animals and spirits had to move often to get away from trouble. Slowly they moved up through different worlds until they reached the present one, called the Glittering World.

The first humans, called First Man and First Woman brought light to the universe. They carved the sun out of a large piece of turquoise, then the moon out of a piece of rock crystal.

As the first dawn began, First Man and First Woman found an infant bundled in a cradle made of sun rays and rainbows. They raised the child who became Changing Woman, the most beautiful maiden in the universe. It was Changing Woman who created the Navajo people out of scrapings from her skin mixed with cornmeal.

During the marriage ceremony, the bride and groom wash each other's hands. The medicine man sprinkles corn pollen on both of them in two lines to represent the uniting of two families. The family members then eat a special cornmeal porridge from each of the four sides of a wedding basket. The medicine man reminds the couple always

Rainbow Bridge in New Mexico is sacred to the Navajo and other Native Americans who live in this region.

to seek the help of the Holy People to "keep your feet on the Blessingway."

In the Navajo belief system, the Holy People have great power, but not always for the good. This is a way of recognizing that there is always good and evil in the world, and within each person. While the Navajo do not fear death, they see it as a dangerous time because the spirit may be wandering. A speedy burial returns the deceased person to the four elements from which everything is made— earth, water, fire, and air.

4 · THE PRESENT AND THE FUTURE

The struggles of the Navajo that began in the 1860s continued through most of the twentieth century. Poverty was widespread and emergency government funds were needed to help the Navajo through several severe winters. In 1950 the U.S. Congress passed the Navajo-Hopi Long-Range Rehabilitation Act, which provided nearly $90 million to build schools, hospitals, and roads. Then oil and mining companies increased their activities in Navajo territory and, by 1970 the reservation no longer had to depend on government funds. By the year 2000 nearly all Navajo children were going to school, many continuing on to college.

Today, the Navajo feel that they live between two worlds— the world of modern America and the traditional world of the Navajo beliefs and way of life. As a member of the Tribal

A meeting of the Navajo Tribal Council in the council chamber.

Council said, "The Reservation is like a foreign country within the United States. We are caught between two cultures. Somehow we must borrow from each."

Two Points of View

Steve Randall is a young Navajo who is not pleased with all the changes created by modern life. He did well in school, and he was a star athlete in football and track. But, he says, "where I grew up, we didn't have running water. I hauled water every day. I chopped wood every day, too. It was a challenge and it was fun. Now my little brother doesn't have to haul water or chop wood. He feels useless around the house. Everything today is pushing buttons. It feels like we're losing so much.

But a Navajo businessman disagrees: "We must be part of mainstream American society," he states. "We need modern business. We need jobs and money."

"I grew up on the dirt floor of a hogan. We were so poor

that a Boy Scout trip was a special treat because it meant three meals a day. Today, I don't have to wear a headband and feathers to prove I'm a good Navajo. I can be a good Navajo by running a good trucking company."

The mixing of old and the new, the traditional and the

Many Navajo children have schools nearby, but others must travel as long as an hour to get to school. Some who live in out-of-the-way areas are sent to boarding school.

modern, can be seen in many ways. Driving along a reservation road, you might see a Navajo girl wearing a long dress and a turquoise necklace, tending a flock of sheep. Across the road, a teenage boy in a T-shirt and jeans is rounding up a dozen ponies using a battered old pickup truck. Farther

While some Navajo people still live in hogans, others choose modern homes.

on, a crossroads diner looks like it could be anywhere in America. But the menu includes items like kneel-down bread, Navajo tacos, and lamb stew. You would also notice that some of the people there speak English, others Navajo.

No matter what changes and challenges the Navajo face, their ability to endure, and to keep their culture alive makes them a very special people.

· TIME LINE

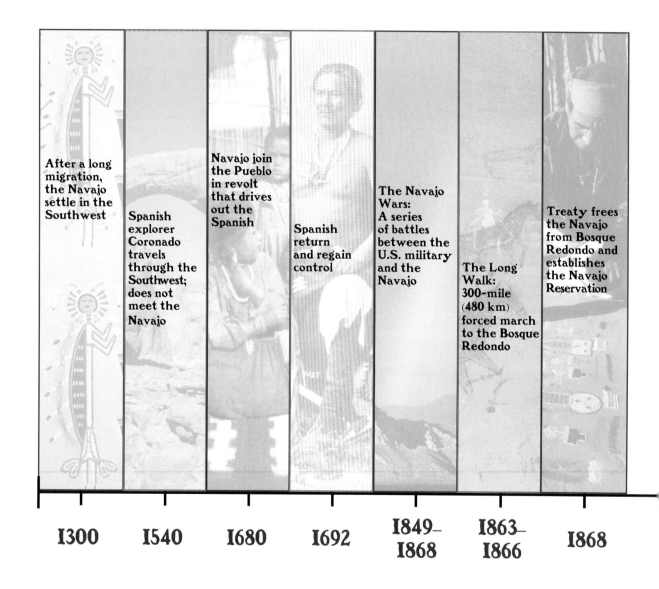

After a long migration, the Navajo settle in the Southwest

Spanish explorer Coronado travels through the Southwest; does not meet the Navajo

Navajo join the Pueblo in revolt that drives out the Spanish

Spanish return and regain control

The Navajo Wars: A series of battles between the U.S. military and the Navajo

The Long Walk: 300-mile (480 km) forced march to the Bosque Redondo

Treaty frees the Navajo from Bosque Redondo and establishes the Navajo Reservation

1300   1540   1680   1692   1849–1868   1863–1866   1868

Navajo children removed from their homes and sent to government schools

Oil is discovered on Navajo Reservation

U.S. Congress grants citizenship to all Native Americans

U.S. Government authorizes $90 million for construction of schools, hospitals, and roads in the Navajo-Hopi Rehabilitation Act

Utah finally gives Native Americans the right to vote. It is the last state to do so

Navajo officially call themselves the Navajo Nation

Navajo establish an office in Washington, D.C., to work for government action on issues affecting the Navajo

| 1871 | 1921 | 1924 | 1950 | 1957 | 1969 | 1984 |

· GLOSSARY

Blessingway: A group of ceremonies designed to create harmony and balance in life.

Bosque Redondo: The arid region where the Navajo were relocated in the 1860s after being forced on the Long Walk by American soldiers.

Changing Woman: A favorite mythical figure of the Navajo. She created the Navajo people.

chantway: A healing ceremony.

Diné: The Navajo name for themselves, meaning "person" or "the people."

Dinetah: The Navajo name for their homeland, located mostly in Arizona.

First Man and First Woman: The mythical beings who rose from the middle earth into the Glittering World, where they found the Dinetah.

Glittering World: The present, existing world to which First Man and First Woman led the earth's other living things, and in which harmony and peace are possible.

hogan: A Navajo house, usually built of logs and a domed roof covered with red mud. There are no windows and a single door faces east.

Holy People: Invisible spirits who can help the Navajo learn how to live properly. The Holy People are not always good, a reminder that there is always evil.

Long Walk: The 300-mile (480 km) journey the Navajo were forced to make to the Bosque Redondo when U.S. troops drove them from their homes in the 1860s.

mantas: Square pieces of cloth worn as shawls.

ramada: A shaded structure made of four poles with a roof of branches, used as a cool, shady shelter from the summer sun; also called a shade.

reservation: Land set aside by the U.S. government for a Native American tribe or nation.

sandpainting: A dry painting used by medicine men in healing ceremonies.

taboos: Actions that the Navajo believe may anger the Holy People.

Tribal Council: First formed in the 1920s, it became the first governing body for the Navajo. Representatives are elected by the clans.

· FIND OUT MORE

Books

Armstrong, Nancy M. *The Navajo Long Walk.* New York: Scholastic, 1996.

Bial, Raymond. *The Navajo.* New York: Marshall Cavendish, 1999.

Bonvillain, Nancy. *The Navajos: People of the Southwest.* Brookfield, CT: Millbrook Press, 1995.

Doherty, Craig A., and Katherine M. Doherty. *The Apaches and the Navajos.* New York: Franklin Watts, 1989.

Sneve, Virginia Driving Hawk. *The Navajos.* Needham, MA: Silver Burdett Ginn, 1996.

Stan, Susan. *The Navajo.* Vero Beach, FL: Rourke Publications, 1989.

Web Sites

Native Americans

www.americanwest.com/pages/navajo2.thm

Navajo Nation

www.navajo.org

About the Author

David C. King is an award-winning author who has written more than forty books for children and young adults, including *Projects About the Eastern Woodland Indians* in the Hands-On History series. He and his wife, Sharon, live in the Berkshires at the junction of New York, Massachusetts, and Connecticut. Their travels have taken them through most of the United States.